WHERE'S MY ANSWER

7 KEYS TO SURVIVING YOUR SEASON OF WAITING

MIKE SMALLEY

Where's My Answer?
7 Keys to Surviving Seasons of Waiting

Copyright © 2009 by Mike Smalley

Unless otherwise indicated, all Scripture references are from the New King James Version of the Bible (NKJV).

ISBN: 978-1-61584-241-4

Hall of Honor

The following made the printing of this book possible. I encourage all who are benefited by this book to call their names in prayer!

Bryan and Casie Fratt
Georgia Thomas
Donna Burton
Darren and Kimberly Bishop
David and Dorothy Spradlin
Anthony and Eileen Pena
Sammy and Mary Pena
Sandra Dinkins
Robyn Collins
Gwendolyn and JW Fields
Paul and Maudie Lawyer
Arlena Sickles
Linda F. Baker
Daniel Pickering
Mauricio and Angela Lastra
Diego and Isabella Giovanna
Mignona Cote
Pastors Glynn and Carolyn Davis

Bonnie York
Mary Jo Brinkley
Fred and Brenda Taylor
Joe Duran
Annie Snyder
Ken Anthony
Christopher Walsh
Sharon Wright
Edith Cantu
Dr. Betty Dlamini
Carolyn Bittick
Sherri Roles
Pastor Curtis Newton
Pauline Harrison
Sharon Strasser
Howard Lull

Table of Contents

Chapter 1
Mastering Life's Ultimate Priority
p. 11

Chapter 2
Remember Your Last Word From God
p. 17

Chapter 3
No Weapon Formed Against You Will Prosper
p.21

Chapter 4
Embrace A Passion For The Word Of God
p. 25

Chapter 5
Personalize The Promises Of God
p. 33

Chapter 6
The Law of Expectation
p.39

Chapter 7
Make Your Seed An Intercessor
p. 43

"People Without A Dream Always Misunderstand The Dreamer."

Dr. Mike Smalley ©

Introduction

Waiting Is Painful!

Waiting. . . for an answer to prayer.

Waiting. . . for a desperately needed miracle.

Waiting. . . for someone you love to change.

Waiting. . . for a financial breakthrough.

Waiting. . . for your gifts and skills to be recognized, celebrated and rewarded.

Waiting. . . for someone you love to see their need of God's forgiveness and reach for salvation found only in Jesus Christ.

Waiting is a Divine School. . . an "in between" place from your past to your future where the Holy Spirit mentors with time-sensitive instructions.

No one avoids the school of waiting.

Waiting forces us to re-examine our beliefs. Our beliefs in God. . . the Bible. . . even our own abilities and inner persuasions.

Waiting forces self examination. . . reflection on past decisions and present relationships.

The impatient view seasons of waiting as a denial of their dream. Many even mistakenly believe they have no role in bringing a season of waiting to completion.

The wise focus their energies on asking quality questions. . . questions that will lead to an exit from their present circumstance.

There are different levels in the school of waiting. Some "classes" take hours. . . others *decades*.

Satan uses extended seasons of waiting to plant seeds of doubt into our mind and spirit.

Doubts about God's promises.

Doubts that miracles still happen today.

Doubts that God even exists or listens.

Jesus Experienced Painful Seasons Of Waiting

- He waited forty days for His next meal while being tempted by Satan in the desert. (Mt 4:2)

- He waited three decades to launch his public ministry. (Lk 3:23)

- He waited a lifetime for His own brothers and sisters to believe in Him. (Jn 7:5)

- Today, He is waiting for billions to recognize and receive His free gift of everlasting life.

Our Journey Together

As a fellow student with you in the school of waiting, I know the disappointment, pain and heartache of waiting for the new season I desperately need and want to enter my life.

As you read this book, may these 7 keys silence any wrong voice in your spirit and fill you with hope and wisdom for your future.

I believe the most productive, anointed and satisfying days of your life are just ahead!

Dr. Mike Smalley

"Your Future Is Too Precious, Your Emotions Too Fragile, And Your Mind Too Complex To Live Life Without A Daily Impartation Of The Joy Of The Lord."

Dr. Mike Smalley ©

❧ *1* ❧
Mastering Life's Ultimate Priority

The Holy Spirit Is The Most Vital Relationship In Your Life!

Deeper than your heart's need for love or your body's need for oxygen is your need to be right with Him. His favor and mentorship are irreplaceable. No human relationship can substitute for a relationship with Him.

During seasons of waiting you don't understand, draw near to the One who understands everything about you.

The Holy Spirit delights in conversation.

He *craves* exchange.

Many have no understanding or interest in a relationship with Him, yet He is the source of everything they are wanting and needing in life.

The Holy Spirit longs to stand beside you as a trusted teacher, comforter and constant companion.

He is not an "it". . . *HE is a person.*

"However, when He, the Spirit of truth, has come, He will guide you into all truth. . ." (Jn 16:13a)

The Holy Spirit has a strong will. He has emotions. He always reacts to *reaching.*

You are not designed to live life without His daily interaction, impartation and influence.

Scripture tells us much about His feelings and reactions.

He works with our memory.
"He will teach you all things, and bring to your remembrance all things I said to you." (Jn 14:26)

He can be grieved.
"And do not grieve the Holy Spirit of God. . ." (Eph 4:30a)

He can be quenched.
"Do not quench the Spirit." (1 Thess 5:19)

He can be resisted.
". . . You always resist the Holy Spirit. . . " (Acts 7:51b)

Or He can be sought after, loved, listened to and obeyed. He longs to be your best friend.

5 Facts About The Holy Spirit

1. ***The Holy Spirit Created You.*** "The Spirit of God has made me, and the breath of the Almighty gives me life." (Job 33:4)

2. ***The Holy Spirit Is The Only One Qualified To Tell You When You Are Saved.*** "The Spirit Himself bears witness with our spirit that we are children of God," (Rom 8:16)

3. ***He Is The Source Of All True Joy.*** "But the fruit of the Spirit is love, joy, peace, longsuffering, kindness, goodness, faithfulness," (Gal 5:22)

4. ***The Holy Spirit Instructs Christians How To Speak In Moments Of Crisis.*** "For it is not you who speaks, but the Spirit of your Father who speaks in you." (Matt 10:20)

5. ***He Decided The Color Of Your Eyes And Skin.*** "For You formed my inward parts; You covered me in my mother's womb." (Ps 139:13)

There Is Nobody Like Him!

The Holy Spirit is never overloaded, requires no sleep, and never has doubts about Himself or you. He is constantly in the mood for conversation. He never grows weary of discussing His Word, His creation or the concerns of your heart.

I believe the Holy Spirit's daily, minute-by-minute, role in our life is the most ignored, neglected, and underestimated blessing in our Christian walk.

Developing a greater sensitivity to His voice should always be the highest priority of your life!

The Holy Spirit Understands Seasons of Waiting

The Holy Spirit knows the pain waiting produces *and the joy it unlocks.*

He has waited generations for individual families on the earth to love His Word. He has waited weeks, months and years for many Christians to simply obey His instructions.

During seasons of waiting, discuss everything with Him. Share freely your frustrations. . . your anger. . . your fears.

Never be afraid to ask Him a multitude of questions. *He is the Spirit of Wisdom.* (Is 11:2)

"Call to Me, and I will answer you, and show you great and mighty things, which you do not know." (Jer. 33:3)

Seasons of waiting should always produce private moments with the Holy Spirit.

Listen in His presence more than you speak.

Following His instructions leads to the room of answers!

The Holy Spirit works like a master midwife, guiding you through the womb of waiting into the birthplace of your miracle.

Waiting is often painful. . . the Holy Spirit is always your Comforter. (Jn 14:26)

Your daily relationship with the Holy Spirit. . . it's the first thing to remember during seasons of waiting.

Recommended Resources:
For an in depth teaching on God's presence, you'll love my book *10 Master Rewards For Sitting Daily In The Presence Of God* available at *www.mikesmalley.com*

"Every Invitation From God Has An Expiration Date."

Dr. Mike Smalley ©

❧ 2 ❧
Remember Your Last Word From God

God Continually Talks!

Some of the ways He speaks to us are through inner impressions, mentors He sends into our life, and His unchanging Word.

His instructions are always the golden bridge into the future you desire.

When God speaks, there are no wasted words. Every aspect of a word from God is pregnant with divine life waiting to be birthed through your obedience.

God's instructions are trivialized at our peril!

An unnamed prophet in the Old Testament learned this the hard way.

"For the LORD gave me this command: 'You must not eat or drink anything while you are there, and do not return to Judah by the same way you came.'" (1 Kings 13:9 NLT)

Despite a clear command from the Lord and an initial determination to carry out this divine command, the young prophet made a fatal mistake . . . he chose to disregard the last instruction He received from God.

Often, the most dangerous season of your life will be the critical moments between hearing a word from God. . . and taking action to complete it.

In the economy of God. . .obedience is vital.

One of Satan's favorite methods to sabotage a believer is to bring confusion into our life through a wrong voice.

An example of this is recorded in the following verses, when the young man intercepted an old prophet.

"He said to him, "I too am a prophet as you are, and an angel spoke to me by the word of the LORD, saying, 'Bring him back with you to your house, that he may eat bread and drink water.' But he was lying to him. So he went back with him, and ate bread in his house, and drank water. . . When he was gone, a lion met him on the road and killed him. And his corpse was thrown on the road. . ." (I Kings 13:18-19, 24)

The young prophet destroyed his future by deciding to put more confidence in the words of a man than in the last instruction he received from God.

Your future is always decided by your reaction to the last instruction God gave you.

Inventory anything missing from your life. Revisit the last instruction God gave you.

Have you respected it?

Have you meditated on it?

Have you obeyed it EXACTLY as it was given?

Seasons of waiting demand seasons of introspection. . . seasons of reviewing.

Never dismiss the possibility a delay may not be God's denial, but an indication you have overlooked or ignored a strategic part of the receiving equation. . . *His last instruction.*

God is always serious about His instructions being followed.

Obedience leads to the banquet room of divine reward and speeds the delivery of your answer.

Remembering. . . and *obeying* God's last instruction builds a bridge from your present valley of waiting to the miracles and answers you've been passionately pursing!

Stay focused.

Keep listening.

Practice obedience.

Reviewing and implementing your last God instruction . . . *it is the key to what's next in your lifelong journey with Christ.*

Recommended Resources:
You'll love my book *How to Jumpstart Your Prayer Life* available at *www.mikesmalley.com*

❧ 3 ❧
No Weapon Formed Against You Will Prosper

Warfare Is A Normal Part Of The Christian Life!

Warfare within your own mind.

Warfare from the demonic realm that continually assaults our life and those we love.

Warfare from the human enemies of the Gospel who despise the Christ life within you.

There will never be a day in your life you will not experience some level of warfare.

Natural or supernatural. . . known or unknown.

During seasons of waiting, your mind and your spirit will be incredibly sensitive to what is presently missing from your life.

Your mind will continually document to your spirit the length of time you have been waiting.

Waiting often over-magnifies pain, frustration and loss.

Your mind, if allowed, will easily enlarge your present season of warfare and waiting.

Inventory Every Invitation To Battle.

The reward for warfare must be greater than the cost of the battle.

Never waste your mental energy on the mundane, the irrelevant . . . *the unnecessary.*

"Finally. . .whatever things are true, whatever things are noble, whatever things are just, whatever things are pure, whatever things are lovely, whatever things are of good report, if there is any virtue and if there is anything praiseworthy —meditate on these things." (Phil 4:8)

During your seasons of waiting, continually encourage yourself by quoting aloud the wonderful promise from Isaiah:

"No weapon formed against you shall prosper, and every tongue which rises against you in judgment You shall condemn. This is the heritage of the servants of the LORD. . ." (Is 54:17a)

The middle part of this verse, in the Amplified Bible reads ". . . this [peace, righteousness, security, triumph over opposition] is the heritage of the servants of the Lord. . ."

God never promised us a life without warfare.

God never promised our enemies would stop forming weapons against us.

He did, however, assure us no weapon formed against us would prosper!

See. . .the big picture. **Daily.**

Time is merely the equation the Holy Spirit uses to lead your enemy into a sea of humiliation and defeat!

Divine Reward

God is the Master Rewarder of the Universe!

According to Philippians 4:9, there is always a divine reward for keeping your mind world pure, confident and focused!

"Practice what you have learned . . . and the God of peace – of untroubled, undisturbed well being – will be with you." (Phil 4:9 AMP)

You are an overcomer!

You are a winner!

You are victorious!

Your enemy is defeated. . . *not you.*

Seasons of waiting allow the Holy Spirit to showcase the stupidity of those who thought they could destroy you!

Master. . . the art of waiting.

Draw. . . from the well of perseverance.

Outlast. . . your present season of warfare.

Remember. . . God has big plans for you!

Your enemy is weaker than you know. You are stronger than you have yet discerned. Agree with God today. . . *No weapon formed against you will prosper*!

❧ 4 ❦
Embrace A Passion For The Word Of God

Your Reaction To The Bible Often Decides Your Exit From Difficult Seasons Of Waiting!

The goal of all Satanic attack is to ultimately produce doubt in your mind about the Word of God.

Every believer experiences seasons where the habit of returning daily to the Bible is difficult.

Your mind will continually wage war against the Word of God.

"But the natural man does not receive the things of the Spirit of God, for they are foolishness to him; nor can he know them, because they are spiritually discerned." (I Cor 2:14)

In seasons of waiting, your mind will often clash with your spirit, as you seek answers, comfort, and direction from the Word of God.

The Holy Spirit **always** reacts to a desperate cry

to renew our passion for His Word.

It is a prayer He loves answering!

God's Universal Love Letter

Thomas Watson, the great Puritan pastor said, "Read the Scripture, not only as a history, but as a love letter sent to you from God."

While experiencing a season of great warfare many years ago, I wrote a song to the Holy Spirit expressing my heart's cry.

Renew my passion for your Word.
Renew my passion for your Word.
Please correct. . .align. . .
   this stubborn heart of mine.
Renew my passion for your Word.
©Mike Smalley Music

God's Word Is Fascinating!

The Holy Spirit is the most creative writer in the universe. His words are alive, powerful, and life changing. They never return to Him void. (Is 55:11)

Consider the following ways the Holy Spirit uses His creation and ordinary everyday things to teach us the power and benefits of His Word.

The Bible and Its Symbols

1. **Light** –"Your word is a lamp to my feet and a light to my path. . . The entrance of Your words gives light; It gives understanding to the simple."   (Ps 119:105, 130)

2. **Fire** - "Is not My word like a fire?" says the LORD. . ."(Jer 23:29a)

3. **Water** – "That He might sanctify and cleanse her with the washing of water by the word." (Eph 5:26)

4. **Food** – ". . . I have treasured the words of His mouth more than my necessary food." (Job 23:12b)

5. **Honey** – "How sweet are Your words to my taste, Sweeter than honey to my mouth!" (Ps 119:103)

My Favorite Poem

Invitations to minister have taken me to over 25 nations of the earth. The most consistent physical object in any hotel room around the world is the gift Bible placed by the Gideon's International.

The following is a portion of my favorite poem about the Word of God found in the front of most Gideon Bibles:

"The Bible contains the mind of God.
The state of man, The way of salvation
The doom of sinners
And the happiness of believers.

Its doctrines are holy.
Its precepts are binding.
Its histories are true.
Its decisions are immutable.

Read it to be wise.
Believe it to be safe.
Practice it to be holy.

It contains light to direct you.
Food to support you.
Comfort to cheer you.

It is the traveler's map, the pilgrim's staff, the pilot's compass, the soldier's sword, and the Christian's charter.

CHRIST is its grand subject.

Read it slowly, frequently and prayerfully. It is a mine of wealth, a paradise of glory and a river of pleasure."

Gaining Strength

Seasons of waiting for answers often give birth to seasons of emotional, spiritual and mental weakness.

When this occurs, borrow a master secret from the prophet Daniel.

". . . when he spoke to me, I was strengthened. . ." (Dan 10:19b)

Your mind and spirit were designed to be renewed by God every 24 hours.

Hearing the Word of God daily is the single most important habit you will ever develop.

"So then faith comes by hearing, and hearing by the word of God." (Rom 10:17)

5 Ways To Maximize Your Daily Bible Habit

1. Purchase The Bible On CD Or Mp3 And Listen To It Daily.

"So then faith comes by hearing, and hearing by the word of God." (Rom 10:17)

2. Read At The Same Time Each Day.

Psychologists have said for years anything done 21 days in a row becomes a habit.

3. Choose A Translation You Enjoy.

Your mind will beg you to return to a place of pleasure. Select a translation to which you are excited to continually return.

4. Set Reasonable Goals.

Never set a goal to read twenty chapters a day until you master the habit of reading three. When our goals are unreasonably high, we often become overwhelmed by the guilt of not completing them.

5. Never Allow Unwelcomed Distractions To Rob You From Your Time In God's Word.

Reading and listening to the Bible will often result in unexpected interruptions and distractions. Don't let anything or anyone pull you away from the greatest habit of your life.

Where's My Answer?

Never allow Satan to become successful in extinguishing the fire of your passion for God's word.

Wisdom. . . must be pursued.

Answers. . . are the fruit of reaching.

Strength. . . is the reward for time in His Word.

God's Word, when applied, never fails!

The Bible is your master faith energizer during seasons of waiting!

"When I Let Go Of Something I Never Intended To Give, God Lets Go Of Something He Never Intended To Keep."

Dr. Mike Smalley ©

❧ 5 ❦
Personalize The Promises Of God

God Always Keeps His Promises!

Your faith walk will require a constant reviewing of the covenant promises of our Heavenly Father.

What you keep hearing, you keep believing!

A great strategy for self encouragement during seasons of waiting is to quote Bible verses aloud.

Never trivialize this master habit.

I encourage you today to find at least 3 promises in God's Word that apply to your season of waiting. Memorize them. Quote them aloud. Master the power of saying them in the first person or inserting your name.

Example:

"For I know the plans I have for (Your Name)," says the LORD. "They are plans for good and not for disaster, to give (Your Name) a future and a hope." (Jer 29:11 NLT)

The same verse personalized would read:

"For God knows the plans He has for *me*. . . They are plans for good and not for disaster, plans to give *me* a future and a hope." (Jer 29:11)

Standing With You

Every week, our office receives numerous prayer requests. We count it an honor to join our faith with those who trust us with the burdens of their heart.

The following is a collection of promise scriptures representing the most common needs we are asked to pray over.

Remember, in any area for which you are waiting on the Lord. . . *personalize the promises of God!*

Healing

1. "But He was wounded for our transgressions, He was bruised for our iniquities; the chastisement for our peace was upon Him, and by His stripes we are healed." (Is 53:5)

2. "For I will restore health to you and heal you of your wounds,' says the LORD. . ." (Jer 30:17a)

Finances

1. "And you shall remember the LORD your God, for it is He who gives you power to get wealth. . ." (Deut 8:18a)

2. "Honor the LORD with your possessions, and with the firstfruits of all your increase; ao your barns will be filled with plenty, and your vats will overflow with new wine." (Prov 3: 9-10)

3. "Bring all the tithes into the storehouse, that there may be food in My house, and try Me now in this," Says the LORD of hosts, "If I will not open for you the windows of heaven and pour out for you such blessing that there will not be room enough to receive it." (Mal 3:10)

4. "Give, and it will be given to you: good measure, pressed down, shaken together, and running over will be put into your bosom. For with the same measure that you use, it will be measured back to you." (Lk 6:38)

Answers To Prayer

1. "Therefore I say to you, whatever things you ask when you pray, believe that you receive

them, and you will have them." (Mark 11:24)

2. "Until now you have asked nothing in My name. Ask, and you will receive, that your joy may be full." (John 16:24)

3. "For the LORD God *is* a sun and shield; the LORD will give grace and glory; no good thing will He withhold from those who walk uprightly." (Ps 84:11)

Wisdom

1. "If any of you lacks wisdom, let him ask of God, who gives to all liberally and without reproach, and it will be given to him." (Jam 1:5)

2. "That the God of our Lord Jesus Christ, the Father of glory, may give to you the spirit of wisdom and revelation in the knowledge of Him," (Eph 1:17)

Strength

1. "I can do all things through Christ who strengthens me." (Phil 4:13)

2. "And he said, "O man greatly beloved, fear not! Peace be to you; be strong, yes, be

strong!" So when he spoke to me I was strengthened. . ." (Dan 10:19a)

Never under estimate the power of listening to yourself quote the Word of God!

Christians for centuries have found new hope and strength while speaking the Bible aloud during the darkest moments of their life.

God's Word works in every generation!

Turn your mouth into a weapon!

Speak the Word of God over your circumstance!

Personalizing the promises of God. . . it's the faith habit Satan fears the most!

"Guilt Will Tear Down What Faith Has Built."

Dr. Mike Smalley ©

❧ 6 ❧
The Law of Expectation

Words Reveal Expectation!

Need. . . does not decide what comes toward you.

You will always attract what you expect. . . not what you need!

". . . According to your faith, let it be to you." (Mt 9:29)

What you believe is reflected in your speech.

Do you view yourself as worthy of a miracle. . . a financial harvest. . . a fantastic marriage?

In seasons of waiting, do your conversations betray a hidden belief system currently robbing you from your answer?

Have you blamed the devil?

Have you blamed others?

Have you wondered if your past disqualifies you from the future you're dreaming of?

Do answers always seem to elude you?

Is it possible you have simply judged yourself as unworthy and delayed your own answer?

If an atheist recorded your words over a 24 hour period, would he hear faith . . . *or doubt?*

Our words are often deciding God's reactions to us. "Death and life are in the power of the tongue. . ." (Prov 18:21a)

Your Position In Christ

Though Christians acknowledge God has forgiven their past sins, many believe their imperfections make God unwilling to bless and promote them. Many subconsciously believe they are unqualified for the answers and blessings they seek until they are "perfect" or have passed through a "long season" without failures.

While obedience to God is vitally important, your *worthiness* to receive from Him is never based on your performance. . . but on your position. . . in Christ.

"But now in Christ Jesus you who once were far off have been brought near by the blood of Christ." (Eph 2:13)

"If you then, being evil, know how to give good gifts to your children, how much more will your Father who is in heaven give good things to those who ask Him!" (Mt 7:11)

If you see yourself as victorious, you will attract victory. If you see yourself as strong, you will attract strength. If you see yourself as defeated, you will attract failure.

During seasons of waiting, keep your expectation high. Deal ruthlessly with doubt and fear.

Remember the woman with the issue of blood in Mark 5? Despite being broke and exhausted after 12 years of *waiting* for an answer, she had not lost the willingness to reach!

"When she heard about Jesus, she came behind Him in the crowd and touched His garment. For she said, "If only I may touch His clothes, I shall be made well." (Mk 5:27-28)

Never allow present circumstances, the negative speech of others, or your own doubts to extinguish the fire of expectation in your life.

Miracles still happen!

God still speaks. Answers come!

God responds to the expectation of His children.

He is still the God of the impossible! He delights in giving His children the desires of their heart.

"For with God, nothing will be impossible." (Lk 1:37)

Expect your faith to attract answers.

Expect your mountains to move.

Expect an exit from your present season.

The Law of Expectation. . . it's the divine magnet attracting God's involvement in your present season.

&~ 7 ~&
Make Your Seed An Intercessor

Every Seed Has A Voice!

People overlook, ignore and often dismiss their Seeds. *God never forgets a Seed!*

When we plant a Seed with faith and expectation, it never stops crying out to God for the privilege of fulfilling its purpose. . . **and the only purpose of a Seed is to produce a harvest!**

A Seed is *anything* you willingly release from your life. Love is a Seed. Time is a Seed. Patience is a Seed. Money is a Seed. Discretion is a Seed. Advice is a Seed. Prayer is a Seed.

A Seed unsown is powerless on the earth. An unplanted Seed lies in the shadows of greatness unable to birth a miracle. . . a harvest . . . or an answer.

In the Bible, Seed offerings are always very important to God. A careful study of scripture reveals great men moved the heart of God when they presented offerings to Him during times of desperation.

King David

During a season of intense trial for Israel and David personally, he prepared and presented a Seed offering to the Lord.

A plague had killed over 70,000 in a matter of days. *David knew desperate times required desperate faith. . . determined reaching . . . and dedicated sowing.* God responded to David's prayers and the offering he presented.

"And David built there an altar to the LORD, and offered burnt offerings and peace offerings. So the LORD heeded the prayers for the land, and the plague was withdrawn from Israel." (2 Sam 24:25)

What Impresses God?

Giving does not impress God.

Everything God created continually gives.

It is impossible for a person not to give. You only choose what . . . and to whom.

Even evil gives.

Terrorists *give* their children as suicide bombers. Rapists *give* money to charities. Satan *gives* shame, guilt and destruction.

Even in nature, giving is mandatory. The flower gives its scent into the air. The sun gives forth heat and light. Even plants and trees must give forth oxygen.

Since everything in the universe, by nature, must give, what is it about our offerings that touch the heart of God?

Answer: Sowing a Seed offering with the expectation of a harvest requires our faith. . . *and it is the faith part of our giving that pleasures God!*

"But without faith it is impossible to please Him. . ." (Heb 11:6a)

When you *remove faith* from the giving equation, God is no longer pleasured by the offering. When you sow Seed into good soil, with faith and expectation, it is impossible for Him not to be pleased and respond with a harvest!

When desperately seeking an answer, use your faith like a hammer to shatter the walls that bar you from entering the room of your future.

Talk To Your Seed

During seasons of waiting, continually plant Seeds into the work of God. *Always* wrap your faith around your offerings and give them an assignment. Talk to your Seed. Tell it where you are expecting your harvest.

Jesus told you to speak to "your mountain" in order for it to be moved (Mk 11:23). *Your Seed, like your mountain, has ears and is awaiting your instruction.*

Wrong Understanding of Selfishness

Despite the Bible's repeated promises for a harvest, many have believed the lie it is "selfish" to give expecting anything in return.

Are all God's promises meant to believed, trusted in and applied? Of course!

Is a sinner "selfish" if the only reason he prays for forgiveness is because he wants to be forgiven?

Are the sick "selfish" if the only reason they ask for healing is to be well?

It is never selfish to take God at His word! He promised the lost could cry out and expect forgiveness. . . He promised the sick could ask and expect healing. . . *He promised we could plant Seed and reap a harvest!*

"Give, and you will receive. Your gift will return to you in full—pressed down, shaken together to make room for more, running over, and poured into your lap. The amount you give will determine the amount you get back." (Luke 6:38 NLT)

According to the above verse and many others, it is not only *right* to give expecting a harvest, it is *wrong* if I sow without the expectation of a harvest!

When I sow without expecting to reap a harvest, I am documenting my belief God does not keep his word. Doubt will always deny you what God longs to bring you.

Any child of God can take a Seed, wrap it in faith, and aim it into their future like an arrow in the hands of a mighty warrior. Your Seeds will talk to God, continually attracting His attention.

As in David's day, God often brings seasons of waiting to a close just after a precious Seed, wrapped in faith, is released to Him.

Breaking The Back Of Poverty

I'll never forget it!

While sitting in the presence of God in a phenomenal conference, the Holy Spirit nudged me to plant a special Seed of $1000 into the ministry of the conference host.

I had learned some years before something happens when I sow a Seed of $1000 that does not occur at other levels. Many who have sowed at this same level into our ministry have given the same testimony.

(If God ever impresses you to sow a $1000 Seed, count off 90 days and watch what He does!)

I had prepared my Seed and was waiting for the ushers to serve me when the man of God went back to the pulpit and said these words, "The Holy Spirit has just shown me there are five people in this room He will speak to about sowing a second Seed of $1000."

Instantly, the Holy Spirit gave me an "inner knowing". . . *I was to be one of the five.* My heart began to race as I "explained to the Lord" I had just written a check for $1000 and had not even placed it in the offering plate yet!

Sowing the first $1000 had not been a struggle. Sowing a second one within 5 minutes of the first was very difficult.

I have learned and am learning that God never speaks to me about what is in my hand unless He's looking at what is in His.

Nothing leaves Heaven until something leaves the earth.

I planted both Seeds that day and stood up to leave the building. I was alone and no one but the Holy Spirit knew what I had sown. Before I arrived at my car, someone called my name. I turned as a woman thrust an envelope into my hand and walked way. I opened it in my car. It was a check for $1000! I was thrilled. . . until I realized this couldn't be my harvest!

I had simply been given my second Seed back.

I reminded the Lord I had obeyed Him, and according to His Word, I had a right to a harvest! Jesus promised a 100 fold return (Mk 10:28-30).

The First Wave Came In 72 Hours

During this season of our ministry, we were on daily nationwide radio. Our most expensive station was in New York. The air time was over $200 per broadcast.

Three days after planting my Seeds, our ministry office received a call from this radio station. They explained they had been listening to my broadcast. It was new and refreshing, and they were excited over its content! They went on to say, "Every once in a while, we like to do something nice for our broadcasters. Your invoice this month of $4,400 has come to our attention. We've decided to mark that invoice, "Paid in full!" The also announced they were going to play my show on a sister station FREE.

In less than 72 hours, I had received $5,400, and that was just the beginning of my harvest!

What if I had kept the $2,000? There is not a doubt in my mind the radio station would have billed us for the $4,400. . . and all the other harvests I experienced from those Seeds would have never entered my present or my future.

The Seeds you present to God are the photographs He has of your faith in His ability to be your trusted source.

When you are discouraged, mentally drained and physically exhausted, your Seeds are not!

They continually speak to God on your behalf begging Him for the privilege of returning to your future multiplied as a harvest! (Lk 6:38)

Time And God Are On Your Side

Remember in seasons of waiting, time is always a part of the receiving equation.

"While the earth remains, **Seedtime and harvest**, Cold and heat, winter and summer, and day and night shall not cease." (Gen. 8:22)

Our memory is subject to failure.

God NEVER forgets a Seed!

Sowing For a Desired Harvest

The power of sowing a Seed for a desired harvest is truly amazing!

Several years ago, I began to hear from couples unable to conceive a child. Their letters, phone calls and emails touched my heart. For some, their season of waiting had been years. . . with no results.

From the human and medical perspective, every option to conceive a child had been exhausted.

I felt led of the Holy Spirit to instruct some of them to present a "battle Seed" to the work of the Lord, while writing the words "healthy baby" on the left of their check. The following is one of several emails of its kind we have received.

". . . Around nine months ago I sent in a prayer request for a baby after having 3 miscarriages. You asked me to sow a seed and to wrap our faith around that little one and believe for a miracle. We did that and now we are pregnant!" M. & A. Abrahams

Since receiving this email, I now proudly display in my office precious pictures of her TWINS!

Why not prepare a battle Seed today for what you are facing? God is no respecter of persons!

Your Seeds of Faith will instantly begin working on your behalf, bringing you a harvest!

Never view seasons of waiting as permanent seasons of denial. In every circumstance of life, always remember and cling to the promise of Jesus in Hebrews 13:5, *". . . I will never leave you nor forsake you."*

You can create any future you want with your faith and a Seed. *Start today!*

Allow the wisdom keys presented in this book to provide you hope and strength for the answers and miracle breakthroughs you are pursuing.

The devil is a liar.

The joy of the Lord is your strength!

The blood of Jesus still cleanses from sin, and God's promises to you will never expire!

You are taking an incredible journey with the King of the Universe. Hold your head high and smile.

God has an answer with your name on it!

"For I know the thoughts that I think toward you, says the LORD, thoughts of peace and not of evil, to give you a future and a hope."

(Jer 29:11)

Have You Invited Christ Into Your Life?

The Bible says, "For all have sinned and fall short of the glory of God." (Rom 3:23)

Sin is breaking God's law - breaking His commandments.

Have you ever lied, lusted or disobeyed your parents?

Man's standard is very different from God's. Consider the following verse from Scripture:

"For whoever keeps the whole law and yet stumbles at just one point is guilty of breaking all of it." (James 2:10 NIV)

No matter how hard we try, we cannot erase our past sins against God.

The good news is Jesus promised, ". . .the one who comes to Me I will by no means cast out." (John 6:37b)

Will you turn from sin and ask Jesus Christ into your life right now?

When we turn from a lifestyle of intentional disobedience to God and put our trust in what Christ did at the cross, God gives us the gift of everlasting life.

Pray this prayer:

"Jesus, I've known right from wrong all my life. I have chosen wrong. I have sinned. I need a savior.

I repent and turn from a life of disobeying you. I invite you to come into my life and forgive me of all my sins. I confess with my mouth that Jesus Christ is my Lord and Savior. Fill me with your Spirit. I will read your Word daily and obey what I read.

In Jesus' Name, Amen."

If you have prayed this prayer and desire to learn more about following Jesus, please contact me so I can send you information that will show you what to do next and how to grow as a believer.

Attention: Mike Smalley
Worldreach Ministries
P.O. Box 99
Rockwall, TX 75087
mike@mikesmalley.com
www.mikesmalley.com

About Mike Smalley

- Preached his first public sermon at the age of 14.
- Graduated from Southwestern University in 1992.
- Pastored near Dallas from 1992-1998
- Began full-time evangelism at the age of 30, which has continued since 1998.
- Has started over 45 churches overseas.
- Spoken to more than 4,000 audiences in 25 countries, including Asia, East Africa, the Orient, and Europe.
- Noted author of 10 books, including, *Saved Soul Wasted Life*, *10 Master Rewards for Sitting Daily In The Presence Of God, 7 Questions You Must Ask Yourself Everyday and How to Jumpstart Your Prayer Life* and more.
- Hosts the worldwide daily Internet Television broadcast, "Wisdom for Achievers."
- Has appeared on TBN, Daystar, LeSea and numerous other television network programs.
- Has embraced his assignment to *Preach The Gospel To The Lost And Equip Christians In The Wisdom Of God*.
- Is Founder and President Of Worldreach Ministries, based in Rockwall Texas.

Join World*reach* 1000 Today!

My Dear Friend,

I don't believe it was an accident God connected you to this book. I have asked the Holy Spirit for 1000 partners who will plant a monthly Seed of $66 to help me spread the Gospel across the earth. (66 represents the 66 books in the Word of God.)

Will you become my Monthly Partner in the World*reach* 1000?

Your monthly sponsorship Seed of $66 will not only impact millions across the earth, but will also create a personal harvest back to you.

3 harvests you should expect:
1. Divine Health (Psalms 41:1-3)
2. Divine Favor (Luke 6:38)
3. The 100 Fold Return (Mark 10:28-30)

Yours for Wisdom,

Evangelist Mike Smalley

P.S. Log onto www.mikesmalley.com and visit the online store to enroll in the *Worldreach 1000*. Or, you may call 24 hours a day 1-866-96-SOULS. Be sure to request your special partners appreciation gift pack, full of my books and teaching CDs.

One Final Thought

If this book has changed your life, I'd love to hear from you!

Additional copies of this book may be ordered for a friend, small group, or co-workers on your job.

Remember nothing changes people like the Wisdom of God!

Quantity Discount Price List:

Where's My Answer?
7 Keys to Surviving Your Season of Waiting
(B-08)

Quantity	Cost Each	Discount
1- 9	$10 each	None
10-49	$7 each	30%
50-249	$6 each	40%
250-999	$5 each	50%
1000 & up	$4 each	60%

WISDOM FOR ACHIEVERS TELEVISION

Watch Mike teach LIVE every

Monday – Thursday

on Internet Television!

To view a *broadcast schedule,*
join the *LIVE teachings,*
or watch *archived broadcasts,*
visit our website at:

www.mikesmalley.com

NOTES

NOTES

NOTES